Get In! How to Market Yourself and Become Successful at a Young Age

Dan Harbeke

ScarecrowEducation
Lanham, Maryland • Toronto • Oxford
2003

Published in the United States of America
by ScarecrowEducation
An imprint of The Rowman & Littlefield Publishing Group, Inc.
4501 Forbes Boulevard, Suite 200, Lanham, Maryland 20706
www.scarecroweducation.com

PO Box 317
Oxford
OX2 9RU, UK

British Library Cataloguing in Publication Information Available

Library of Congress Cataloging-in-Publication Data
Harbeke, Dan, 1982–
  Get in! : how to market yourself and become successful at a young age
/ Dan Harbeke.
    v. cm.
  Contents: Getting your foot in the door — Networking — Advice from
the wiser — My advice.
  ISBN 1-57886-031-8 (pbk. : alk. paper)
  1. . 2. Vocational interests. 3. Vocational guidance. [1. Vocational
guidance.] 1. Title.
HF5381.6 .H37 2003
650.14—dc22   2003013812

Contents

Foreword

From the first time I met Dan Harbeke I knew I had come across a young man who knew where he wanted to go in life and sensed that he would be in control of how to get there.

As a teenage neighbor, Dan appeared focused, organized, and courteous and carried on with a definite purpose, whether it be to execute neighborhood jobs for small amounts of money, or for the purpose of organizing and coordinating people for competitions like basketball tournaments. I was always struck with the sense that there was more purpose to everything that Dan did than what appeared on the surface.

This book is written to help motivate and direct young people who have the desire to move forward with their life and career with some degree of control. Use the ideas presented here as a guide to take you from a point in your young life without direction along a path you can control. Many of you will be leaving school where, for the large part, your life was organized and directed by others. Your curriculum was chosen and family and friends influenced sports and extracurricular activities. All time schedules were given to you, and you were driven here and there by family and others. As the time comes for you to leave school and make a career choice for the rest of your life, you will want to be able to control your course. It is hoped you will find the subject matter of this book helpful and rewarding, written by someone who is "doing it."

While opportunity waits around many corners, you need to seek it out. It is not often that opportunity comes after you. If you want to get ahead, and move in the right direction, do something about it and control your direction.

So here it is. I hope *Get In!* stimulates understanding, self-examination, action, and results. Use this guide as motivation to take charge and become proactive in controlling your activities and contacts in making intelligent choices for your career and life satisfaction.

— *Bruce Clapham*, president, Charleswood, Inc.

Preface

The idea for *Get In!* came to me while I was working at the Chamber of Commerce of Fargo Moorhead. I became further excited about the writing of this book through the conversations that I have had with many young and older people alike regarding how they have achieved success or how they initially got started. This book is to be read as a continuation of those conversations—conversations that would begin at about fifteen minutes and end up being an hour or more in length.

Get In! encompasses everything that I have learned from my business and work experiences. Those experiences cover a wide range of work, including mowing lawns and shoveling snow in my West Fargo, North Dakota, neighborhood; working at typical minimum-wage jobs, a grocery store, retail clothing stores, the Chamber of Commerce of Fargo Moorhead, the Greater Omaha Chamber of Commerce, and New York Life Insurance Co. These experiences have allowed me to view the skills necessary to thrive in everything from the food business to the retail sector. Through these jobs and internships, I learned the value of hard work, determination, self-sacrifice, independence, and time management. It is all about taking those skills and applying them, as you build your career and enter into the world of business, that will eventually lead to your own personal success.

This book is intended for a younger audience that has goals and would like to know how to achieve them. This book is further intended for those who would like to gain the knowledge necessary to network successfully. *Get In!* is not intended, however, to be an "end-all-be-all" book. It is simply what you would hear me say if we were to have a conversation on the subjects of networking and getting one's foot in the door. This book on achieving business success caters to a younger crowd that others do not in that it is written with youth in mind from a youthful perspective. There are many books on the market today that tell the "seven ways to do this" or quote the "ten proven methods for achieving that." That is all fine and good, but these are directed and marketed to those persons already established in the marketplace. My book is different in that it is geared specifically to those coming out of high school and out of college, not to those who are currently in the job market. However, if someone in the market does read this book, they will surely find this information helpful and will probably have wished that there had been something like this when they were just starting to get their foot in the door. For those of you who are in the market, don't let that stop you, though; this book makes a great gift for those youth in your life to whom you wish the best in success.

Now is the time to learn, develop, and use the strategies mentioned in this book to market yourself and become successful at a young age in order to get in and stay in.

Acknowledgments

There are so many people who have influenced me and helped to shape my life. I would like to take a moment to thank them and the organizations that made *Get In!* possible.

Thank you to everyone at ScarecrowEducation for seizing my idea and making it a possibility. Thank you especially to Dr. Tom Koerner and Cindy Tursman, who worked with me and helped put this book on the shelves and into the hands of those who are looking toward a life of success.

Thank you to Rocco Marano for putting me in contact with ScarecrowEducation and being there when the time came for me to embark on this endeavor.

A huge amount of thanks to my brother, Mark Harbeke, who helped with the initial editing and provided continued encouragement.

Many thanks to those who took it upon themselves to read the initial manuscript and provide me with feedback so that the end result of this book is the best that it can be—namely Stacey Ackerman, Nick Akers, Jason Bergstrand, Brian Bestge, Mike Biewer, David Black, Linda Brakeall, Swanie Brandt, Sadie Breidenbach, Gale Cameron, John Campbell, Bruce Clapham, Shannon Dahl, Al and Mary Hisley, Lola Salmonson Holland, Sven Jasinski, Jill Konrath, Sheila Koser, Kelly Maas, Don Mengedoth, Jill Olson, Betty Opheim, Brady Otterness, Trish Oyos, Tracy Powell, Erin Prochnow, Tricia Remus, Ben Scheeler, Kathy Scott, Justin Senger, Chuck Simpson,

Paul Tefft, and members of the Delta Pi chapter of Alpha Kappa Psi professional business fraternity.

I would like to thank those who held conversations with me regarding success in both business and personal life—namely Justin Johns, Brandon Mason, Devon Moylan, John Pryor, and Greg Tehven.

I would like to thank all of my former employers, most notably the Chamber of Commerce of Fargo Moorhead for providing me with the opportunities to get my foot in the door and work with such wonderful people. Words cannot express how grateful I am for the chance to share ideas, learn, and make a difference.

I would like to thank the band New Found Glory for providing music that I find motivating and upbeat, in much the same way that their music has helped me to view my own life; many thanks to Jordan, Chad, Steve, Cyrus, and Ian.

I would like to especially thank my parents, Bill and Geri Harbeke, for always being there and allowing me to set goals and make possible my dreams. May we continue to share in the joy of family and the love that surrounds it.

Part 1
Getting Your Foot in the Door

Personal Resources

When looking at where you want to go in life and in pursuing personal success, you have to first look at what you have. That is, you have to look at your personal resources.

Personal resources are the things that are all around you: your friends and family, where you live, organizations you are in, and where you go to school, work, and play. When looking at personal resources, think of your parents. Maybe your dad works for a bank or your mother for a nonprofit organization. These can be *huge* when it comes to personal resources. Many times young people have a lot more than they realize. But it is realizing that fact and then making those resources work for you that will lead to your success. When you find the resources you have around you that no one else has, that is when you can go to work.

A lot of times when we are young, we couldn't care less about what our parents do or have done. But that is strictly the point I am making. Asking your parents what they actually *do* and how they came to be where they are today can be an invaluable resource and asset. For example, when I was young, I was the son of a bank president. I had no clue what that meant. All I knew was that my father had the big office in the bank. It was not until recently that I began to ask and wonder what it was like to be the president of a bank. Keep in mind, however, the job title or position of a parent is not everything. There are many avenues and roads to be explored in all positions and fields of business, medicine, volunteering, and

3

commerce. There are some things a textbook cannot teach—those specific instances that happen all the time. That was what I was after. Now that I have had the time to sit down with my dad and pry into him a bit, I am amazed by the wealth of knowledge that resides there. This is just one example of making personal resources work for you.

Using personal resources is a great way to get your foot in the door. As I said, you already know a lot of people in a lot of places, and those people know people who know more people. Basically, you *do* know a lot of people, despite what you may have thought. After establishing those who you know, you can then begin to target those who will propel you most to where you want to go in life, or at least find out early on which avenues you do *not* want to take.

How to Talk the Talk and Walk the Walk

Now that we have established who you know and what personal resources you have, it is time to hone in on those people. Heck, it can even be people you don't know. That is all part of the fun. Make it a game to see how many people you can meet. It proves beneficial as you go along.

Say that you are interested in banking or finance as a possible career. Maybe you just want to know what a business is like, aside from that which you already know. How do you get in? It is as simple as making a phone call. Say that you want to find out more about consulting as a career. Look up some consulting firms and ask for fifteen minutes of the head consultant's time. Take the head consultant out for breakfast or coffee. With any luck, they will buy because they see your ambition. What helps a lot in this situation is to do some research before you start calling. Maybe find a couple of banks, if you are interested in banking, or use your personal resources to guide you in the right direction. Through your research you can find out who the head honcho is—or anybody else for that matter. You can narrow your search indefinitely. Then just move from there, give 'em a call. Say you're so and so and that you are interested in their field and that you would really like to hear what they have to say.

People love to talk about themselves and tell you all that they can. Sometimes they reveal quite a bit, also. They can warn you about what to be aware of and even how to get into their respective fields. The sky is the limit with what you ask and what you hope to find out.

Do not be afraid.
— BRUCE CLAPHAM

The Kid Next Door

One obstacle to achieving personal success is failing to recognize one's personal resources. A story comes to mind about the "kid next door," which illustrates doing just this. This kid has it all and he does not even know it. The kid is a senior in high school and lives in a pretty posh neighborhood. His father is the president of a large chain of banks and his mother works in the offices of a nationally well-known insurance, financial, and consulting services organization. Right there you would think this kid would have his ear upon many doors of opportunity, but, unfortunately, this is not the case.

The kid has so many resources that many would beg for the opportunity to have, but he fails to recognize them, let alone use them. Just imagine whom this kid could have access to if he only wanted it. If he were interested in banking, he would only have to ask his father. If he were interested in basically any facet of business, chances are that his parents would know where he could go, whom he could talk with, and what he should do. The sad thing is that this one story matches so many out there who have the resources, but fail to recognize them, let alone use them.

He who tastes not, knows not.
— RUMI

Doesn't Everybody Want to Be a CEO?

So what about everyone else? Doesn't everyone want to be successful? One would hope so. But doesn't everyone want to be a CEO or a president? The answer is no.

I recall asking my dad the same question and he told me a story that related to his career in banking. It was about this man, Ted, we'll say, who was an agricultural lender. You could have offered Ted the job of president and he would have turned it down with a smile. Was he capable of being a bank president? Certainly, and probably more so than most. But Ted found his passion in agricultural lending. He enjoyed both agriculture and the lending aspect of banking. He enjoyed driving out to the farmstead and talking with farmer Joe just as much as he enjoyed doing the work that was necessary back at the office. He was content with his own. For Ted, doing agricultural lending *was* the same as being a CEO or president.

So, not everyone wants to be CEO or president. What does that mean? Well, a lot of things, but for one it means a little less competition on your way to the top. Another thing is that people want different things in both business and personal life, and it is being respectful of that, while being mindful of getting your foot in the door when and where others aren't willing to go.

Never, never, never, never give up.
— WINSTON CHURCHILL

Meeting Mr. Cameron

There was one occasion when I was looking into consulting firms in the Omaha area and found one by the name of Greenwood Performance Systems. I had obtained the necessary contact information through the Greater Omaha Chamber of Commerce website. The fact that Greenwood was a Chamber member was a plus with my already-established Chamber background.

I proceeded to search the Internet and found quite a bit of information on the company. I found out that Greenwood had offices throughout the United States, besides the one that I was researching in Omaha. As I viewed Greenwood's website, I gathered information on what the company did, whom it catered to, the different types of consulting it did, who the company leadership was, the company's mission, how it became established, and so on. I then went one step further and had Greenwood send me its company information. Not only that, but I found a name that I could contact as well. It was that of past Vice President Gale Cameron. I received a number to reach him at and planned to call his office the next day.

So it was, that on the following day, on my way to work at the Chamber at 7:30 A.M., I called this number, expecting to reach a secretary and possibly leave a message for Mr. Cameron. Much to my surprise, though, the voice that came over the phone answered not by saying, "Good morning, Greenwood Performance Systems," but simply saying, "Hello?" I was taken aback by this and proceeded to ask for Gale Cameron. The voice responded that it was actually he who was on the other end of the line. I was so freaked out that I had accidentally called the man at home that I nearly drove off the road—and with that being said, there is one caveat of using cell phones while driving.

When I regained my composure, I introduced myself and apologized for calling him at home, as I was under the impression that I would be calling his office. I further explained that I was interested in consulting and was currently a student attending Creighton University in Omaha, Nebraska. I also mentioned that I worked at the Chamber and that when I returned to Omaha, I would like to go out for coffee sometime and discuss consulting and how he got into it. From there we closed the conversation—as I was at that point rolling into the Chamber parking lot—and I would from then on look forward to receiving more specialized company information from him personally, as well as sharing in conversation with him upon my return to school in the fall.

I must say that it felt really great to receive company information a week later at my house with an enclosed personal letter from Gale pertaining to our phone call. That was one connection that I value having made in that I learned a little bit more about the consulting business and now have someone from whom to personally garner more information. And all of this happened in a very short while having just looked up something I was interested in, making a few phone calls, and taking the initiative. Not too tough and very beneficial.

Meeting Mr. Mengedoth

Don Mengedoth is a man I am very proud to have met. Don has done many things in his life, most notably affecting mine would be his work with Community First Banks, as my dad was past president of the Wheaton, Minnesota, branch. Don not only started Community First Banks (CFB), but was also president and CEO of Community First, as well as past president and chairman of the board for the American Bankers Association (ABA), and is now working hard in Colorado.

It turns out that I had wanted to meet this man for quite some time. I probably had in the past, but surely I did not recall it, as I was much younger when my dad was in banking. Well, it just so happens that Don's lake cabin is not too far from ours in the lakes country of Minnesota. My family had actually driven by it many times on our way to and from restaurants around the Detroit and Pelican lakes area.

So, one Friday after working all day at the Chamber, I was planning on going to the cabin for the weekend, as was most often the case with my weekend plans. But this weekend would prove a bit different. I figured that since I was already in a suit and tie, what better time to drop by his cabin to say hello and introduce myself. So, I drove to the lakes that Friday after work and pulled into the driveway of his lake house. I walked up to the front door and was greeted by his wife. After asking for Don and telling her that I was Dan Harbeke, Bill Harbeke's son, she invited me in and proceeded to get Don.

I was in awe of their lake house and the fact that I was getting the opportunity to meet *the* Don Mengedoth. Don came in from the dock and gave me a firm handshake that I will not soon forget and greeted me with a smile that only a man who has achieved such life successes can. I said that I was in the area and figured it was due time that I come over and introduce myself. We chatted about my family and what my dad was up to as well as *his* future endeavors and what it was like to be involved with the ABA and banking in general. I soon let him go, out of respect for him and his food on the grill, as both of us, I am sure, wanted to enjoy what was turning into a beautiful weekend.

I have never left a place with a high such as that. It was quite the joy to see my dad the next day and say that I just *happened* to run into Don. He was amazed and I was thrilled. And now because of that I have the opportunity, whenever I call upon it, to call, e-mail, or write Don. Maybe it will be for a holiday greeting, to ask advice in business, to proof a manuscript, or whatever else that I may wish to ask of such a person. But it is the fact that I took the initiative to make that initial connection. Sure it helps that Don knew my dad, but it had been a long while since they had spoken. Also, the fact that our lake cabins were close did not hurt.

This meeting was bound to happen in due time, but it is taking that initiative to get up and go. It is looking for those "ins" and taking them when you have the chance. Looking at your resources—be it having a parent or relative who knows someone; living near or knowing someone who lives near someone of business influence; or just finding out for yourself where you have to go, who you have to meet, and how you have to do it—will set you well on your way to not only getting your foot in the door, but also kicking down that door altogether. But the important thing is that you do it.

Could I have met Don and made this connection without having had these resources? Sure. It might have taken a different approach or required finding common ground by other means, but it would have happened had I wanted it to, and it will happen if *you* want it to.

> *The purpose of life is to live it, to reach out eagerly*
> *and without fear for newer and richer experiences.*
> — ELEANOR ROOSEVELT

A Little Goes a Long Way

When meeting people such as Don Mengedoth, it is pretty cool to think that there are a lot of people out there—a lot—who know who he is, what he does, and so on. But a lot of those people never get the chance to meet the guy. Maybe they receive a company memo or stock prospectus with his name somewhere within, but surely it is not every day that people can say they met the man. For example, people might have worked for CFB for *years* and not known him personally, whereas in ten minutes on a warm and sunny Friday afternoon, I was able to make a connection. That is using one's resources, and it feels pretty good. It is a feeling and drive that will only push you further in achieving success in both business and personal life.

Meeting Mr. Simpson

Chuck Simpson is another man whom I made it a priority to meet during my summer at the Chamber. Chuck is president of Business Growth International (BGI), a prestigious consulting firm located in Omaha, Nebraska, that focuses on the growth of medium- to large-size firms on both a national and international scale, with one of the most notable being ConAgra Foods.

I went about finding information on BGI much the same way as I researched Greenwood Performance Systems. I then sent a personal letter on Chamber letterhead, in a Chamber envelope, with the address of BGI printed on a Chamber address label; I inserted my Chamber business card (Dan Harbeke, Project Assistant) and a copy of the Chamber's award-winning newsletter, *The Bridge*, in which I was featured for joining the Chamber during the summer months. I figured since I had the means to keep things consistent with using "everything" Chamber, I might as well.

Before I wrote the letter to Chuck, I researched the company and again had its information sent to me. It was quite easy, as their website had a place where one could enter a name and address to receive company information rather anonymously. After I read through the information and decided that this would be something up my alley, I proceeded to meticulously write my letter. I kept things formal and to the point. I mentioned who I was, where I went to school, and that I was interested in the field of consulting. Heck, who better to ask for advice in that field than a consultant? I further mentioned that I would soon be returning to the Omaha area for school and that I would like to meet sometime for lunch, or morning coffee, to talk about the business of consulting. I also asked whether the company had a formal internship program. It never hurts to ask.

Not too long after the letter was sent, I received a reply. It was from the president of BGI, Chuck Simpson himself. Yes! The letter went on to say that he would enjoy getting together upon my return to school in the fall. Double yes! Regarding the internship opportunity, he stated that though they did not have a *formal* internship program, he did take on an intern nearly six years ago who was now doing "very well." Although I was indifferent on the internship opportunity, it did spark my day to know that there was an opportunity to work with this man in or out of the office, albeit a small one.

When I returned to Omaha that fall, sure enough, we got together for breakfast. I dressed business casual and arrived shortly before him and his partner, the former intern, at the downtown location that we had chosen per our phone call a week prior. I met for an hour with both Chuck and his partner, Sven, as we discussed how both of them came into the business and how they came to work together. It really is a phenomenal story that would take an entire chapter in itself. I asked questions and did a lot of listening. What was nice was that they, too, asked questions about what I wanted to do in business and in life, what I was doing now, and what I have done in the past. I found out that Chuck was from Minot, North Dakota. I had a resource that I was not even aware of. He also went to Dartmouth College in New Hampshire for a portion of his undergraduate as well as graduate education. It just so happens that I know another man who is president of a men's formalwear shop in Fargo who attended Dartmouth and whose son also attended Dartmouth. This man's son was even on Dartmouth's men's crew team in the varsity lightweight four. I, too, am in crew and a member of the men's varsity lightweight four. Who knew?

Aaaahhhh, the connections are amazing, especially when they begin to overlap. I did not even have the chance to see if Chuck and the men's formalwear owner know each other. Did I mention that the North Dakota governor, and his father, also went to Dartmouth?

There might come a day when I want to get my MBA and gee, guess where I would like to go? It never hurts to know some alumni. Huh, wow, the possibilities.

Great things are done when men and mountains meet.
— ANONYMOUS

"It's on Me, Kid"

What is so often the case when going to lunch, even when I am the one who presented the invitation, is that the meal is often paid for by the person I am taking to lunch. Although I always have my wallet ready and am willing to pay, the person I am meeting more often than not pays for the meal. So, not only are these occasions beneficial in providing a free meal, so too are they beneficial for what they provide in connections and information. I prefer the latter, of course, no matter who pays for the meal. The offer is what is important.

The Truth of the Matter Is . . .

When consulting your resources, you will most likely find that it is not a problem for those people to set aside some time for you, either over the phone or in person. The truth is, people like to talk—about themselves, their work, their families, how they got to where they are today, and so on. People like to talk, and they will.

Surround yourself with challenging people and ideas.
— ANONYMOUS

Research Smesearch

When looking up companies, as I mentioned previously with my examples of BGI and Greenwood Performance Systems, it is vital to look at a company from all angles and perspectives. There are so many ways to research a company, it is crazy. If only more people utilized these methods, they would not find themselves stuck getting internships, or even careers, in fields that they dislike.

Trade journals, such as the *Wall Street Journal*, are wonderful sources of daily information on business happenings and issues in commerce. The emergence of online news distributions has risen dramatically in recent years and further proves to be an excellent source for gathering information about companies and the current business climate. It should also be known that the stock market serves as a plethora of knowledge and information, which largely tends to be unbiased. It certainly never hurts, either, to catch fifteen minutes or more of a headline news program during the day or evening.

In life there are efforts and results, and the strength
of the effort is measured by the result.
— ANONYMOUS

"I Know Something You Don't Know"

The easiest way to research a company, assuming that you know very little about the company, is through the Internet. Companies, no matter how large or small, often have a website. Search the company and look at numerous website listings that pertain to, or mention the company. Look at sites that rank certain companies and see if your targeted company comes up. Look to see if the company has a "request information" section. Boom, then request some information. Look to see who the decision-makers are in the company, who the president is, who the head of a department in a field of interest to you is, and so on. Look at everyone and take down their names and personal contact information if you need to.

Continue to research the company once you receive their hard copy of information and facts. This is also a good opportunity to see if the way the company gets back to you is professional and fits your personal style. Also, one thing to keep in mind when requesting information is that the company has no idea who you are. In their mind, you could be a prospect, another company who wants to do business, a current client, or anything else along those lines.

If you want to succeed and you prepare to do so,
you will achieve your dreams.
— ANONYMOUS

The Ws

Find out what the company does, what market it's in, why it's in business in the first place, who it caters to, how long it has been in business, who is in charge of those decision-makers you looked up, who the company's clients are, and so on. Ask yourself, do you know the clients, the companies, the people who work there? Do your folks work there, a friend's parent, or anyone else you already know? Read through the website material in the areas of interest to you. The worst-case scenario is that you will find that the company is not up your alley and that you can move on to a new company and not waste anyone's time.

Look Who's Talking

Another method for researching, aside from the already-mentioned Internet and hard copy company information, is to talk with those who work for the company or have worked for them in the past. It does not matter whether you know or do not know anyone who works for the company. This might be a time when you call upon one of the names that you wrote down. It could be the president, a department head, a secretary, or administrative assistant. This is a good avenue to take before deciding whether it would be beneficial for you to traverse bigger waters. Give this person a phone call or send him or her a quick e-mail. Keep it brief with your questions serving as the main focus. Again, they may not need to know everything about you, but it might be beneficial to say that you are a student, or otherwise, simply requesting information on a more personal level. Take note, however, that this step works best after you have researched the company enough to go on and take the next step.

Say What?

When talking with these people via the phone or e-mail, ask questions such as:

- What is it like to work at this company, or for so and so?
- How long have you worked at the company?
- Why did you join?
- Why did you leave?
- What is the growth potential?
- What are my chances for personal advancement?
- What is the atmosphere?
- What type of personality fits the job profile?
- Is this a company that you would recommend for someone with my abilities, education, or interests?
- What do you *not* like about the company, or so and so?

The range of questions can really be your own—and should be. The important thing to keep in mind is that you are talking to one of the best sources because they actually work, or have worked, for the company. However, take note that it is beneficial to talk with more than one person in more than one area to avoid that one person who might have had a bad day or is otherwise frazzled about something.

1 ... 2 ... 3 ... Contact

O nce you feel comfortable with the information you have received, for as many companies that you have requested information from, it is time to contact those companies whose people you have either already met or spoken with, or those who have sent you their contact information. Even if you have trouble obtaining the information for that person you wish to contact, send a letter to the company address targeted to that person. However, this is where it helps to have spoken with those in the company to find out just how to go about contacting your target. Keep in mind also that the smaller the company, the larger the availability of possibilities for you to make an impact once in the door.

Wherever you go, go with all your heart.
— CONFUCIOUS

Draft a Target Letter

Draft a target letter. That is, write a letter to the person who is in charge, or is the decision-maker. This is where you state who you are and what it is that you want; of course, not so blatantly. When writing the letter, you may simply state that you have taken it upon yourself to research the company and then state what it is that you are targeting. Maybe it is an internship. Maybe the company does not offer a formal internship program and, with the information that you have obtained on the company through your research, you now see a place within their organization where an intern could help and, gee, guess who the perfect person would be to take on that position? You!

Someone's Done Their Homework

Maybe there is something else—a problem perhaps—that you have noticed through your research that you could shed some light on. Write the letter in such a way that states that you have done your homework, that you have noticed something, and that you have a way to fix it, improve upon it, or get around it. For Pete's sake, do not tell them right then and there, but suggest that if they want to find out your solution, you would be willing to meet to discuss it. What is that person going to say? "No. I don't want help in this area or I am not interested?" Maybe, but that is rarely the case. That decision-maker will want to hear what you have to say. Show them that your thinking and ideas have promise. Yeah, if you do this, that's right: you just got your foot in the door. Man, it feels good! Who knows, maybe they will like your idea or maybe they won't, but at least you got in and made the contact. If they do like what you have to say, then maybe they will take you on for the short term to address the problem. From there, they may take you on permanently if your work shows promise and truly does make a difference. This is just one of many ways to get in.

Today is the best preparation for what tomorrow may bring.
— ANONYMOUS

The Big No-No

One method that students take on when attempting to get their foot in the door is the mass mailing. I will tell you this does not work, flat out, bottom line, uh-uh, no-no, don't do it! That is, the student sends out a hundred or so resumés, or otherwise-related materials, to a hundred companies. They are not going to get the career they want—maybe a job—but certainly not the desired career.

Don't always follow the crowd because
nobody goes there anymore.
—YOGI BERRA

"So This One Time, at the Registrar's Office . . ."

One day during my freshman year of college, I was in the registrar's office picking up a transcript for this, that, and the other. While I was waiting in line, this guy in front of me—no joke—orders a hundred transcripts. His plan, as he made clear by talking with the secretary behind the desk, was to send out one hundred resumés with one hundred transcripts to one hundred companies. Man, oh man, I tell you, what a waste. This "ready, fire, aim" strategy is not a good one to follow. I am sure that this guy never achieved his desired career path, or at least delayed his attainment of this by many years. Wow.

Aiming isn't hitting.
— ANONYMOUS

Resumé

Having a resumé from the beginning helps immensely in building your career early. I can tell you, however, that it is important to do what you think is best and to showcase that which places you in the best, most honest light possible. Recently I had the opportunity to look at resumés posted by a local Omaha university. These resumés all had the same format with the same five phrases listed under a section titled "Summary Qualifications." Surely these qualifications fit the profile of somebody, but certainly not everybody. The problem was that everyone had the same five phrases written down. For goodness sake, if you read a "how to" resumé book, use it for a reference, not verbatim. Don't use a book to tell you how—you know how. Something that will never hurt is bringing a copy of your resumé to your parents, teachers, and your other personal resources to garner their feedback. You may not always agree with or appreciate what they have to say, but chances are they have traversed the same waters in their day and know the ropes. They might just have something good to say and something to add or change that could make all the difference.

Some think it is appropriate to use a resumé program on a computer, while others think it is best to use a simple word processor document. With either method, be certain to keep the information current—update it frequently—and if you think you can back it up, then put it in. If you are a confident person, let your resumé reflect that. However, do not let confidence turn into arrogance.

Presentation is everything. Go out and purchase some finer paper. Don't shy away from even using the kind with the watermark. Doing so will make an impression, and a positive one at that. Furthermore, some say it is good to keep your resumé at one page, others think resumés should be two pages long. I would suggest that you really only need one page containing all the good stuff. However, the position for which you are applying also holds some weight in that it might, at times, be a wise idea to put in a little more information that could be pertinent to that position. Use your good judgment and you will be ahead of the game before you know it.

Interview

Sweaty palms, dry mouth, and a bit shaky in the hello. It's okay; it's an interview. It's normal. One piece of advice, however, is to carry a portfolio. Sure, it sounds like a stock term, because it is. But a portfolio in this sense of the word is typically a leather-bound folder looking thing, which is perfect for carrying extra copies of a resumé, business cards, and a legal pad for taking notes. If you go into any office equipment and supply store, they will certainly know what you are talking about. The portfolio is a great, not-too-expensive business tool. As far as the interview itself goes, there are some wonderful titles listed at the end of this book that will be better able to shed light on this subject specifically.

Getting in Does Not Always Mean Getting Wet

Okay, so maybe the company did not like your idea, or they did not return your target letter. Oh, well. There are a lot more companies out there. You would hope that, in your initial research, you would have distanced yourself from a company where you would have fallen into such a trap. Making those initial connections help so much when you later *do* send that target letter. However, you know you're doing well in getting your foot in the door when you do not need a target letter at all to get in, but they just invite you in because you are who you are, and you have proven that.

Also, if you do receive that internship or project proposal because you believe that you can help, and it does not prove to be everything you wanted, that is okay. At least you know what you *don't* want to do. There have been many tasks within my own internship experiences that had me question why and where this was helping both the organization and myself. But in the end, it always seems to roll together, make sense, and provide better and more opportune situations for you down the road to success.

You must act as if it is impossible to fail.
— ASHANTI PROVERB

Correspondence What?

Correspondence is HUGE. It is letting those people whom you have met with, regarding whatever, know that you appreciated their time and consideration concerning whatever it was that you were meeting about. Correspondence is also vital if you received an internship, career opportunity, or some otherwise-stated opportunity.

You should always take the time to drop notes when there is apparent appreciation on your part. E-mail might be all right for some situations, but handwritten correspondence is where it's at. This is especially true when dealing with interviews, lunch dates, and simple thank-yous.

1. Promptness is key when dealing with such situations.

2. Sending any form of correspondence has a little more clout and garners more appreciation when sent within a few days to a week of the action rather than a month or two. I believe that you should send it the same day.

3. It is important to keep your correspondence short and to the point.

After the Interview

After an interview, it is very important to drop some form of a thank-you note, either designated to the person who interviewed you or to the organization as a whole, depending on the size of the organization and the individual context of the interview. You should always hand-deliver the correspondence if possible, as that, too, carries with it a certain degree of care and appreciation. However, it has been proven an effective means of correspondence for the interviewer in certain cases to thank the interviewee. It certainly feels good to receive some form of a thank-you from the company that you are interested in, but it feels horrible if they send correspondence and you do not. Ouch. Keep on your toes and you will be able to avoid this folly.

Whuddaya Say?

So, what do you say when writing such correspondence? Keeping it short and sweet is usually a good start. Thank the person for the interview, lunch, or whatever kind of meeting it was, as well as for devoting time and consideration to your needs. Mention that it was a pleasure meeting with him or her, as well as getting to know him or her better personally and professionally. Say that you will look forward to speaking together in the future and then close with a formal closing such as "Sincerely" or "Regards," or possibly a witty remark such as "Sellingly Yours" or "Yours in Success" if, for instance, the interview was for a career in sales. The sky is the limit on that one, but using your own judgment and caution, or seeking guidance from others, never hurts.

The Little Things

You know, the little things that you do in reference to corre- spondence don't mean a lot . . . they mean everything. It is sending out little notes of thanks, sending a birthday card, giving a small gift just because, calling someone to thank them for their advice on a past issue, or some otherwise related event that neces- sitates some small form of appreciation. In light of this I am re- minded of the quote "Dance with the one that brung ya." That is, for example, if someone takes you to lunch, thank them by doing something more than just saying thank you. If someone gives you advice, a ride home, a summer internship, or a career opportunity, be certain to thank them in one way or another. Something that I like to do, that is simple and very effective, is sending a thank-you, but not with the generic thank-you card you might find at your local grocery store or gift shop. It really makes a difference to go to a Successories type store and pick up some blank motivational cards. Then when you write to the person, you can match the card with the occasion, the person's personality, or anything else that seems to fit. There have been many occasions that I have sent a card containing a nice moti- vational message with a golf background to a mentor who plays golf, or a card with someone's favorite quote on it with simply a thank-you message enclosed. Sure, it makes sense to do these things, but that is just it. You would be amazed at the number of people who overlook this simple, small task. The little things don't mean a lot, they mean everything. Trust me.

Part 2
Networking

Be There

One big thing, at any age—but especially at a young age—is being around. Be present. Make the appearances. It pays off to do so in both professional and personal settings. There are countless occasions that you can place yourself in such a location to get noticed. Maybe it is reading a business book or doing your homework at a coffee house or bookstore; or showing up to a conference, meeting, or even a party with your friends. Chambers of commerce often times offer wonderful networking opportunities with events such as "Business After Hours," "Coffee and Contacts," or even "Chamber Cafés." Making appearances at both business and personal functions is vital. If you find it difficult to attend such events, simply consult your resources or ask a friend. All you have to do then is play dress up and knock 'em dead . . . or at least it should seem that easy.

"What'f I Don't Wannuuu?"

In personal settings, you should *want* to go because your friends are probably there or it will be fun, but you should also find good reason to go if these instances are not the case. The important thing is that you recognize events and situations where you can make an appearance and at which those of importance to you will be present. Who knows who you will see at such events? I have attended many events where I thought it would be a disaster, or at least not fun, but more often than not, I have been surprised to find someone of influence to make my day, night, weekend, or even year. By going to these conferences, parties, church events, and so on, you set yourself up to see a lot of people. But think also of all those who will *see you* without you even knowing it.

Basically, make the appearance even if you might not see it fit in with your short-term goals. Think of all those students, kids, adults even, who aren't doing *this*, or going to *that*. You instantly have a leg up on them, and because of this you are really going the extra mile. However, in these cases, don't just go the extra mile, go ten miles.

Living Life in the Glass House

When making the appearances and playing the networking game, however, keep in mind the "glass house" that you are living in. It is very important, especially at a young age, to realize this point. The point is that there are so many people who see you, and will continue to see you, without you even knowing it. Sure it is crazy to think about, but that is why it is important to always be on your best behavior and to put on the best face possible—because you never know who is watching. Those people watching could be waiting to tear you down at your first faltering step or, on the other hand, waiting to promote or hire you the next time you prove yourself successful.

First Timers

So, it's your first time to a networking conference, eh? That's okay. Here are some helpful hints to make it an occasion you will want to attend again and again. First things first: Survey the room and get your bearings. See who is attending, where a familiar company booth is located, where the food and drink are located, and even look for someone else who might appear lost or shy. You might be surprised what they have to say or offer to you. If you are not comfortable going it alone, however, or if you know absolutely nobody there, that's all right; simply ask a friend to attend with you. That is, of course, a friend who has either networked before or knows a few people at the place you plan on attending. Chances are your friend will know a lot of people, be willing to introduce you around, and talk you up at the same time. Tagging along with someone, or having someone tag along with you, can be quite beneficial and can better prepare you for those times that you *will* be going it alone. However, be aware of "cling-ons," as they can detract from your appeal. These people add no value to you and your approach, but always seem to be around. The key is to go with someone who is complementary to your qualifications and interests. Quite often, you can simply call on one of your personal resources who is "in the know" to help you out. They will most likely feel obliged and willing to make the effort to further your career.

Listen

When you are at a networking conference or trade show convention, it is important when speaking with people that you listen. Gee, that is a no-brainer, but it is huge. The best way to garner information from someone is to ask questions. Simply ask the person what he or she does. Heck, what do *you* do? Be sure that you know and are ready to answer. You will surely get a few minutes worth of feedback that will allow you to either ask more questions or simply carry on the conversation as it ensues. By asking questions of the other person, it will help you to remember more about him or her while making them feel important at the same time. It almost sounds too good to be true, but that is most often the case—just you wait and see. Also, by asking such questions, you will be able to identify who will better aid you in your efforts to get your foot in the door.

A Case of the Wandering Eye

One condition to be aware of, however, when speaking at such a venue is to not have a wandering eye while carrying on your conversation. Keep eye contact with the other person, or persons. If you do not know what I am talking about, keep your eyes open at your next networking opportunity. These people are easy to spot. They carry on conversations while moving their eyes about the room to seek out their next victim. I can assure you that this is very rude, and equally not effective in terms of networking. A lot of respect can be lost over something as small as not keeping simple eye contact during a conversation. When networking, you will have to distinguish whether you are the type who talks to everyone but does not remember a thing, or the type who talks to a few people but remembers everything. See where you fit in and how you can improve your skills.

So now that you have their eye contact, what do you say? If you are a student, mention what you are studying. Ask them what they studied? Ask them for advice. Follow the list of questions in the "Say What?" chapter. Talk about the venue of the conference or convention. Discuss the food or businesses that are present. You may find that some people want to talk your ear off while others will seem to have left their manners at home and only care about how many stacks of papers are on their desk back at the office. Many friends of mine have received internship offers, many times at places that traditionally did not even offer internships, when speaking with men and women at trade shows, technology conferences, and networking conventions. Go for it and attain and maintain eye contact. The payoff will be worth it.

Hungry Anyone?

So, you find yourself at a networking conference and you notice that huge buffet table. What do you do? Eat, maybe, but be wary. You are there to network, not gorge yourself. Heavens to mergatroid, keep that in mind. Also, just as you kept your eye on the person with the wandering eye, be keen to sense those who are stuffing their faces. Watch them try to network; they cannot do it. Their hands are full with food and drink. How are they supposed to shake a hand or give/receive a business card? Don't get me wrong; the buffet table can be the perfect place to strike up a conversation about what you read in the *Journal* that morning while you're tooth-picking that piece of cheese.

Like a Good Scout, Be Prepared

Just as it is important to make the appearance, keep eye contact, and so on, it is equally important to be prepared when networking. That is, there are certain activities you can do that will make it much easier for you to relate to others in conversation—or simply start a conversation, for that matter. Reading the newspaper is probably the easiest thing a person can do. Right there you will have the tools necessary to strike up a conversation about sports, the weather, or even local and national news. The key is to be up to date on things. Also, if there is a company newsletter that comes out for the function you are attending, take it upon yourself to get a copy and read it. Many chambers also have such publications; it would be wise to take an occasional gander at some of them to keep up to date on business happenings in and around the community. Much like organizational newsletters, the business page in your local paper also carries the most recent career jumps, mergers, promotions, and so on. These can be good starts to any conversation and, in a worst-case scenario, you will at least know a lot more about the business community of which you are a part.

"So This One Time, at Band Camp . . ."

Go to camp. Attending "big grown-up" conferences can often times be difficult for those who are younger. In that case, attend your own youth conference or camp. Attend your American Legion's Boys/Girls State. Go to Hugh O'Brian Youth Leadership conferences. If for whatever reason you are unfamiliar with HOBY, you should find out—you won't be disappointed. Join your school's student council, Key Club, DECA, or whatever else, and attend their respective state and national conferences. You will meet so many people at these conferences, as well as become friends with them. You will have endless contacts from all over your own state and nation, for that matter. Heck, go big, go international. Be sure to keep in touch with these people. It is so easy now because we live in a society where e-mail is extremely prevalent and easily accessible. I can tell you from my own experiences that I have contacts, and good friends— both student and adult—all over the tri-state area, the nation, Australia, Thailand, and Canada. And who says I am stopping anytime soon? Go for it. Join those organizations both in your school and your community. Attend their conferences and keep those networks of contacts and friendships alive.

Position Yourself

Networking largely involves positioning yourself. Positioning, positioning, positioning. I cannot say it enough. Positioning: there, that'll do. That is, by just getting involved with one opportunity or another, you position yourself for future involvement and for those in places of success to see you, and for you to see them.

Positioning has allowed me to get where I am today (wherever that is). It took the involvement of one leadership program to spur everything. From there, student council, Boys State, National Leadership Camp, National Honor Society, International Student Representative Conference, and the list goes on, with conferences to boot. It is taking those first steps—if only small ones—to get you on the right path for where you want to go. Heck, I imagine that you have probably done more than I have, and that is great. But it is so important that you *have* taken those steps and that you *have* taken that initiative to position yourself for future success by what, where, and how you have been involved with opportunities. It is taking those small steps and continuing to take them every day. What steps have you taken? What steps will you take?

Volunteering for and Involvement with
Service Clubs, Organizations, Etc.

I cannot quantify how beneficial it is to be involved or affiliated with service clubs and organizations. There are so many clubs and organizations that you are able to be a part of when you are young. What is great about that is that most of the time those same clubs will hound you for a membership when you *do* get into business and begin to further your career. Talk about a great start to networking.

Also, it is highly probable that your folks belong to an organization or club. Ask if you can attend one of their meetings. Many clubs often have a regular dinner meeting. Go and get a free lunch and shake some hands. Go and meet Mom and Dad's friends and co-workers.

I have had the great fortune to be involved with, but not a member of, the Fargo West Rotary, Jaycees, and other affiliations with groups such as the Cass County Youth Court. Through Youth Court, for example, I met Betty Opheim, who from then on has made it a point to get me involved with the Rotary, which has in turn sponsored me for such things as money to attend an international conference in Australia and is now getting ready for a possible scholarship opportunity to study overseas after college. All that for just getting involved in an organization and meeting the adult members.

You know, your friends and other acquaintances in such organizations and clubs have parents too. What a great place to start gathering those resources and continuing the networking process. It is up to you, though, where and how you choose to volunteer, or get involved or affiliated with clubs and organizations, and who you'll meet along the way. The more you can take on, and *handle*, the more beneficial and fun building your network is going to be.

Volunteerism can take you anywhere.
— DAN HARBEKE

"Here's My Card"

Get a business card. I cannot say how important that is. There have been a few occasions where I have kicked myself at a conference for not being prepared enough to have something as simple as a business card. Go out and spend thirty bucks or less to get five hundred business cards with information as simple as your name across the middle with your address, phone number, and e-mail address at the bottom. Your friends may laugh and be like, "Nice business cards." But pay them no mind; you should be the one laughing because they have yet to realize the importance of having the tools to get oneself in and on the road to success at a young age.

Write on the back of the cards you receive from other people. That is a great piece of advice. Doing this allows for personal cues later on when you need to know why you got their card in the first place. The notes should be used to tell you who they are, what they do, and items such as the fact that they were going to maybe take a vacation or have an internship possibility available down the road. Once you have this readily accessible knowledge, all it takes is a follow-up to ask, "Hey, how was the vacation? Good? Great. So, what was it you were saying about that internship possibility?" Get business cards. Carry a pen. You're set.

Walk Tall

When networking, smile, walk tall, and strut your stuff. Good grief, you should be happy and confident when you are networking because you should begin to realize all the personal resources that you *do* have and how they are helping you more and more every day.

The man of genius is he who finds such joy
in his art that he will work at it come hell or high water.
— STENDAHL

Rolodex: Learn It, Live It, Love It

When building your network, and as you accrue more and more contacts every day, buy a Rolodex and a business-card catalog. Go through them at least once a month and take note of who is, and is not, working out for you. The important thing to ask yourself if someone is *not* working out is, "Why not?" Maybe you need to drop that person a quick note or give them a phone call. Be sure to check up on your e-mail address book as well. You would be amazed at how much easier it is to drop a simple, small note to each person, rather than to draft a huge letter that will be sent to everyone. The former can have a very positive impact, while the latter is totally non-personal and can sometimes be disrespectful.

The dawning of the technology era has spawned increases in methods for compiling and having available the information you need for keeping track of your contacts. The most notable piece of equipment would be that of the personal digital assistant. Granted it might take the mowing of a lot of lawns to purchase such an item, but again, it is certainly a wonderful accessory to have for the technologically savvy.

Networking Pays, and It Shows: A Personal Story

I received my Chamber internship through networking, plain and simple. How exactly, you ask? Well, it did not hurt that I was involved with the Chamber's Youth Leadership program as a sophomore in high school. It was a great program that consisted of thirty-two sophomores and juniors from area high schools who met once a month doing various leadership, team-building, and community-directed events. The program has grown so much in the past few years that two additional classes were added and now the program has found its niche with just two classes. The program offers an opportunity for alumni to return and further develop the program. Boom, I was there. I kept involved for the duration of my junior and senior years in high school doing everything from going to planning committee meetings to facilitating certain sessions and graduation ceremonies. Not only was there a youth program, but there was an adult program as well. I found it very beneficial being involved on both levels.

So, how was it, then, that I came to acquire my internship with the Chamber through this avenue of involvement? I was attending a leadership initiative workshop that I was invited to because the Chamber wanted a youth perspective. Who better to ask than the kid who has been with the program since 1997 and has worked with both adult and youth programs? It was on the second day of this three-day conference that the Chamber president and CEO, John Campbell, asked me what I was doing that coming summer. I had some plans, but nothing set in stone and certainly nothing lined up in the realm of business. As I mentioned my plans (or lack thereof) he offered me the opportunity to work both my Christmas and summer breaks from college. I was thrilled and almost speechless, as the Chamber does not have a formal internship program and the fact that I was asked by the president himself. I accepted.

Getting It Done through Networking: A Personal Story

Networking pays off, no matter your age. I found that out at a young age. I was tagging along at "Business After Hours"—a Chamber-sponsored networking event where many companies gather to promote, mingle, and sell their services in a more relaxed, after-hours atmosphere—with former Professional Development Coordinator Tricia Remus, the head of both the adult and youth leadership programs. I had had an idea for putting together a deep thought/quote book for quite some time, seeing as how I had compiled my own deep thoughts over the years. I was a senior in high school and was looking for something big to do; this book was it.

So, while tagging along and meeting and greeting, I asked Tricia how I might go about this. Right there, the options I had were limitless. She introduced me to Swanie Brandt, who worked for an imaging company. I presented my book idea to Swanie and she liked it. From there, I brought Swanie the compilations that I had received from the members of my senior class and together we worked on what layout would be best. Swanie put in her time on this for no charge at all. I could not have asked for more. We set up many meetings between the two of us, and even one with Gary Meyer, of a local printing company. We were able to select the paper and cover that we wanted and also discussed price. While things were a go in that area, it was up to me to then walk and talk with area businesses to come up with the financing for the book. There again, I was setting up meetings with bank presidents, owners of coffee shops, and community developers. Most everyone liked the idea of a book made by youth, for youth. The fact that they could contribute was all the more enticing. Talk about advertising to a target market! On behalf of their sponsorship dollars, they would be able to hit up more than five hundred people who would be potential customers for, say, opening a bank account, buying a home in the future, or even buying a simple cup of coffee.

Short end to a long story, the book was completed and handed out to more than three hundred graduating seniors, various high school teachers and faculty, friends, and family across the United States, and even some friends overseas. None of this would have been possible without networking. Networking can be something as simple as tagging along at a networking event and asking where to go and who to talk with in order to achieve a certain goal. Not too tough but quite an accomplishment. That is the power of networking at a young age and the payoff that networking can produce.

Coming together is a beginning; keeping together
is a process; working together is success.
— HENRY FORD

Yeah, Yeah, Sure: Networking—So What?

Through the various early networking opportunities that came my way, many of which were through the Chamber of Commerce, I was able to become involved and stay involved with many committees, or otherwise related activities. This involvement sparked an ability and opportunity to make appearances. I was asked on several occasions to facilitate certain leadership sessions and graduation ceremonies. What better way to get your name out there than to actually be out there?

There was one occasion that I spoke as the keynote at the adult leadership graduation. Now, I probably had met a few of the adults that day, or may have even known them prior to that day, but I certainly did not know all of them. The point is that, on that day, and many days afterward, they all knew who I was. It was a pretty cool feeling that when I would be at the mall or catching a movie, or even attending another networking event, adults would come up to me and mention that they had seen me speak at their leadership class graduation. It is all pretty neat stuff for just getting involved, staying involved, increasing my personal resources, and making those appearances.

Part 3
Advice from the Wiser

Five Things to Keep in Mind

During my last week at the Chamber I had the fortunate opportunity to sit down to lunch with the Chamber president, CEO, and friend, John Campbell. Throughout our conversation, I was interested in finding out how he got where he is today and what he thought to be good business and personal advice. He mentioned five things:

1. Don't bed your ethic. Simply meaning that you have your morals and beliefs, and you should stick with them. If there is something that you do not agree with, do not be afraid to speak up about it. Say, for instance, that someone is going about bad business dealings and they want to bring you along for the ride. You know they're bad to begin with, so don't do it, unless of course you want to get caught and throw away everything you have ever worked for. Stick to your guns.

2. Don't chase the dollar. Too many people focus solely on the dollar sign and not on the work that they are doing, or *should* be doing, for that matter. This especially seems to be the case with the young businessperson. Engage in work that you enjoy and that propels you to keep learning every day. Your reward will come in due time.

3. Don't be afraid to hire those better than you. I would like to think that John had this in mind when he hired me. Yeah, right, maybe

someday. By doing this, you will find there are many people who *know* more and can *do* more than you possibly can. That is just the point. Bring these people aboard, in any organization, and do not be afraid to let them shine. After all, you're the one who got them there, right?

4. Treat others as you would like to be treated. That is another way of stating the Golden Rule. If you want to be treated well, treat others well. If you do not want to be yelled at, don't yell at others. If you do not want to have your things stolen, do not steal from others, whether it be ideas *or* material things. It's the Golden Rule, plain and simple.

5. Integrity. Integrity is a word that comprises such traits as honesty, sincerity, firmness in decision-making, and an overall quality of the person. What's not to strive for there?

The Key to Success

Again, during my last week at the Chamber, I sought out administrative assistant and friend, Mary Hisley, for lunch. During our lunch, we talked much ado about something. That something was business success, and how one can achieve it.

Mary asked me what I thought the key to success was. After many minutes of chomping away at my salad and throwing out random thoughts, I had exhausted all the words I could think of, none of which were making the mark she had anticipated. I finally gave up. At that moment, she pulled out a yellow, rubbery-plastic key from her purse that read, "The key to success is self-discipline." There it was. It made so much sense.

That key chain had it right: self-discipline *is* the key to success. She went on to explain that it takes a certain person to stay dedicated to the task, be it getting an A on an exam after long hours of study or getting an interview after pinpointing and using one's personal resources. Self-discipline is doing those little things, but going further to doing them every day. It is getting up every morning to work out, read, make a friend, make a contact, and the list goes on. Keep at it. That's self-discipline.

Father Knows Best

My dad has taught me so much that I thought it would be a good idea to share some of the advice he has given me. My dad grew up in the small town of Page, North Dakota. Just how small of a town is Page? Well, let's just say that he played six-man football in high school. Yeah, that is small.

He is a man who has accomplished much in his life and has done so in being a farmer; agricultural loan officer trainee; assistant cashier and agricultural representative in Langdon, North Dakota; assistant vice president and head of the Ag department in Valley City, North Dakota; president and chairman of the board for Community First Bank in Wheaton, Minnesota, and financial planner for American Express Financial Advisers. He is currently the director of stewardship and development for the Catholic Diocese of Fargo.

Dad on Career Moves

My dad has "been there and done that," but he has always been sure to let his superiors and colleagues know when he intended to move on and why. He also made certain to thank them for what they had done for him and his career. It is important to learn from any and all bosses and co-workers, both in positive and negative ways, because you never know which contact will work out and advance your career. Maybe you can advance his or hers, too, down the road.

Dad on Profit from the Company

My dad said that if you ever have a chance to buy stock in a company, and think it's a good deal, do your best to buy it and keep it. Also, he said that if you ever have the chance to invest in a good situation, consider it. Don't do it automatically, but if the situation is good, you know the business, the facts, the employees, the risk, the potential downside (as well as the upside), and so on, then give it a go.

Dad's Random Thoughts on Business Success

In banking and other kinds of business, make sure that you prepare, work hard, and advance your career success by building bridges, not burning them. Be ready for new opportunities, situations, and moves as—or before—they occur.

Let your bosses and supervisors know you're ready, for a new promotion or otherwise. If you *are* the boss or supervisor, make sure that your employees are already in the know about possibilities for advancement. Be prepared to take "calculated" risks. Swag versus wag. If you find yourself to be unfamiliar with these terms, just ask your folks.

When volunteering, make sure you are serving to serve and not just doing it to network for personal gain. The latter move will show up and cause backlash. Be certain to train, give resources, and let go, while at times keeping an overall perspective on the situation. Respect all people you work with, be task-oriented, and remember that all people are just that—people.

Probably the most important lesson that my dad has taught me, or the one that I remember most, is that one should strive to under-promise and over-deliver. Say, for example, that you tell someone you will have a project done by 2 P.M. Have it done by noon instead. Also, you might be at a restaurant and they tell you that it's a 30-minute wait, but when you get seated in 15 minutes, it feels pretty good. That is what he is talking about and what I am saying.

Dad on Motivation

There are really only three ways to motivate people, in that motivation arises from greed, fear, or vision.

Greed can be used for a while with sales contests, incentives, promised or potential raises, and promotions. But if that is all that is motivating your employees, they may leave you and go elsewhere, or may end up not being very well-rounded people, thus not creating the best long-term employees.

Fear can be a short-term motivator. For example, if they don't get the job done, they won't be around long, or the lowest performer will be fired. But fear is seldom a good, or long-term, motivator.

Vision is the one thing that *can* consistently keep employees motivated to keep performing at high levels to achieve the company's goals. If everyone knows, understands, and believes in the goals, and further believes that they are important and that you can lead them to reach those goals, they will do almost anything to help you achieve those goals.

Dad's Sports Analogy

In any job or organization with which you are involved, remember this sports analogy: Professional athletes, whether in football, basketball, baseball, or any other sport, are extremely well-trained, well-paid, and very motivated people. But every year before the season starts, they go back to the basics of their profession. They train to get into the best condition possible. They work hard on the fundamentals of their sport, even though they have likely been playing it for ten or twenty years. You would think that they could walk right in and play at, or close to, the level they had been performing at before. But that is not always the case as they need to discipline themselves to start at the beginning and get "up to speed" before they proceed. We need to remember that sometimes we need to work on sharpening our basic skills, and add new "basic" skills—such as what happened when personal computers arrived on the business scene—before jumping right into a new job.

Dad on Learning from Others

You can learn so much from others in similar or different companies, and through business organization and service clubs. However, you must "consider the source." Some people will rightly (or wrongly) try to prejudice you one way or another, depending on their own backgrounds, beliefs, or goals. Don't believe everything you hear, especially when it is mostly bad or mostly good.

So That's Who I Get It From

My mother is the epitome of a volunteer. She has worked the part-time jobs and volunteered in all ways imaginable with her heart always yearning to help others. She enjoys nothing more than doing new and different things with different people from different places. My mother volunteered for the American Cancer Society (ACS) for eight years as vice president, and eventually president, of the local county unit when we lived in Wheaton, Minnesota. During her time volunteering she helped to initiate three new ACS fundraisers that were very successful as well as a Senior Citizen Hall of Fame, which honors seniors who have contributed to the community in some way. The hall of fame is still active today, nine years later. She has also volunteered as a district advisor, a liaison between ACS staff and various counties, and worked with the volunteer county board members to share new ideas with each other to take back to their individual boards. These mechanisms for volunteering provided the tools necessary for successful networking.

During our move from Wheaton, Minnesota, to West Fargo, North Dakota, my mother received a phone call from the same ACS staff, asking her to be an administrative assistant responsible for supporting eighteen counties. She was a little skeptical, as she had no knowledge at the time of office equipment or procedures. She was, however, very knowledgeable about the American Cancer Society and what was most important to the organization. Learning the office procedures and equipment would become the least of her worries. She took the job, which was part-time at that time and loved the work. Within three years she was promoted to full-time as the North Central Region assistant to the vice president. The new position allowed her to take the role of support staff for fifty counties in the northern two thirds of Minnesota. Upon taking her new position, my mother also became involved with income development and within three years, helped revive a fiscally struggling county into a very profitable unit, which remains very successful today. She has also brought forth new-found community support for events such as Relay for Life and Daffodil Days, involving local universities and colleges. She could not be more proud to say that she was a part of the process and outcome.

Clearly, continuous volunteering, no matter what stage of life one is in, provides lifelong opportunities. ACS had faith in my mother and because of her volunteering in many areas, she acquired the knowledge of many different people, places, events, and ideas. Her volunteer background led her to a fantastic job where she could still work with volunteers. The work became easy, as she knew how to "talk the talk" with those involved with ACS to move projects and events forward in an effort to get things done. She has formed many friendships all due to volunteering. Volunteering inevitably allows for the building of relationships that one may need in the future.

One final piece of advice my mother always gave me, not quite in relation to volunteering, was to never assume the other person knows what he or she is doing. This could relate to driving down the street or to people in the workplace. What I gather from this is that one should do all one they can to ensure the success of something—an activity, event, or project. Work hard and volunteer, and relationships will be formed and strengthened, allowing for professional and personal success. Thanks, Mom!

Expand Your Horizons

Go away. Certainly come back, but do not be afraid to leave to expand your circle of influence. Depending upon what you have done and where you and yours have been, the world is either large or small. Allowing you to go away to experience life's pleasures allows for hugely different perspectives and opportunities. It is vitally important to continually think beyond the borders and anticipate all that is accessible and free. More important, it is that thinking which will take you wherever you wish to go professionally and personally.

Whether you believe that you can do a
thing or not, you're right.
— HENRY FORD

Part 4
My Advice

Throughout this book, I have given you the tools and techniques that have proven successful for getting your foot in the door and networking, but here are a few more things to keep in mind when going out and getting it done at a young age.

Look Sharp, Be Sharp

G et a nice suit. It is really important when you are starting out that you look professional. If you want the part, start by looking the part. I recall, when walking into places as a senior in high school, not having a suit but still wearing a shirt and tie and thinking I owned the place. It was a pretty cool feeling. It was not cockiness, but a confidence that allowed my shoulders to remain back and my stance to be tall. Heck, when I did get a suit, the sky was the limit.

I still remember the expressions of good taste that spouted from the mouths of those at a Chamber trade show and technology conference the first time I wore my suit. Even though my duty at the conference was only to accept breakfast tickets at the door, it still paid off to look professional and act that way as well. For the rest of the day, I walked around the floor and mingled. I cannot tell you how many times I was asked, "Who are you with?" and "Do you have a card?" Most people were astounded that I was only a freshman in college at the time. It felt pretty good. It is not that tough.

I tell you what, though, when I say that you ought to purchase a suit, I don't mean one of those flashy ones that you would wear to a nightclub. I mean one that you can purchase at a reasonable price from a JC Penney, Marshall Fields, or Von Maur, for example. Women may do as they please in this case, as long as it is a professional business suit. But guys, take my word for it when I say this: Get measured and know your sizes. You will be hard-pressed to find a comfortable, good-looking, respectable suit that says "large," "medium," or "small" on the tag. A nice pair of shoes never hurt anybody either, and they are not hard to find for a reasonable price.

Aim for distinction and you will attain it.
— HENRY DAVIS

Your Worth

Do not be afraid to ask for what you are worth, whether it involves mowing lawns, shoveling snow, or getting into your career aspirations. I'll never forget the time I was shoveling snow for my elderly neighbor up the street when I was in middle school. He was a perfectionist. I happened to mow his lawn as well and it was imperative that it looked—and felt—like carpet. No joke. So, needless to say, this perfectionism carried over to the winter months. On this one day, however, I had shoveled and shoveled and finished just as the sun was setting. Need I remind you of the severity of a North Dakota winter? The older man came out to greet and pay me as I finished up. I asked for $10, as I thought that was both fair and not asking too much. However, he refused to pay until I asked for more. I was confused. He explained that I should not be afraid to ask for what I thought both I, and my work, were worth because it was evident that I had labored for hours and done a fine job. He asked me again for my fee. I thought for quite a while and eventually said that $25 ought to do. He agreed, with a smile, and reminded me to always charge what I believe I am worth. Sure, it is a nice gesture to ask for only so much, but you should not be afraid to ask your worth.

Dollarize Yourself

L earn to *dollarize* yourself. When you are getting into your career, or even an everyday job, for that matter, learn to place value in yourself and your work. For example, if you have a method that will bring in X number of dollars for a company, make sure that you get a certain percentage of that amount. For example, maybe you have a fund-raising idea that will generate $10,000. That's great! Maybe because of your efforts with the project, you would ask that you receive 1 percent, or even 10 percent, for your troubles. That is *dollarizing* yourself and showing your worth to the company.

Doing your research early with a company perspective will shed much light upon this and allow you to take an outside look at the company, thus allowing you the potential to observe any possible problems that the company may be facing and solutions to those problems.

We all have the gift of potential.
— ANONYMOUS

Never Settle

Don't settle for second best, or worse. That is, if you are looking into a company that you think is too big or too good for you, don't let that stop you. Go for it. Don't settle for the little job offer at company XYZ that you *know* you can get. Also, say you are looking at colleges. Go big. Sure you can get into the community college or state school, but if you want to go private or bigger, then go. There are financial aid programs and scholarships for a reason. The payoff will be huge down the road for making such a choice.

Good, better, best, never let it rest, until the good becomes the better, and the better becomes the best.
— SANTA LUCIA RESTAURANT, FARGO, NORTH DAKOTA

24/7

All day, every day. That is when you can be doing these things. It never stops. What matters is when you decide to get in the game and make a difference for yourself, and for others.

Success comes before work only in the dictionary.
— ANONYMOUS

Keep on Keepin' on

When many people engage in these networking and get-your-foot-in-door activities, they begin to think, "Oh sure, I can do this." But what happens most often is that they might do these activities for one day, but what about the next day, and the next after that? More often than not, people become unmotivated because they do not see the fruit of their labor right away. That is why it is important to keep at it. Don't stop, even if one thing goes awry or bad. As the Australians say, "No worries, mate." There is one simple solution, however, that you can enact to ensure that you keep with it and continue your activities. This solution is to simply plan ahead and manage your time. That is, set up appointments for a week from today, tomorrow, or whatever. Set up a lunch date to take place in one month. Sign up for a conference in the spring, fall, winter, or even summer. Plan ahead and manage your time. If you do not have a planner, get one. Not a cheap-o, and not necessarily Dad's "executive plus," either, but something professional that allows you to set appointments and dinner and lunch dates, make contacts, keep contacts, or simply write that you have homework that night. Time management and planning ahead, along with self-discipline, are some of the greatest tools you can use to ensure that you keep on track, and on pace, to setting 'em up and knockin' 'em down.

> *Sometimes I get a little out of hand. I've made so*
> *many friends, so many plans, a million people,*
> *and so much time that I don't have....*
> — NEW FOUND GLORY

Mmm . . . Books

Read books. Look over books. Get a subscription to a highly regarded business magazine or paper. Spend an hour at a Borders or Barnes & Noble by just grabbing five or so books and looking over their main points. You will walk away with so much information. Maybe you did that with this book. Great. Often you will find really valuable information on a variety of business topics and situations. Maybe you will eventually purchase those books. Good; add to your library. From doing these simple things you will be able to gather many short stories, quips, and anecdotes that you can use in conversation or to relate to other people, resources, businesses, goals, opportunities, or whatever.

Multiple Perspectives

Diversify what you read. Sure you will find the authors that you really like or the periodicals that really tickle your fancy, but, as with people, it is important to gather your information from multiple perspectives. Ask your personal resources what they read, why they read them, and where and how you can also read those same materials.

There are also a handful of online newsletters from a handful of consultants. Subscribe to them. Find someone who writes in an area of interest to you. Maybe it is sales. Get an online newsletter subscription in sales. The best part is that these publications are usually, if not always, free. Man, it can't get much better than that.

From the Aisles: A Personal Story

I am reminded of a story that happened not too long ago during my writing of this book. I was looking at a number of publications in the business book section of a local Barnes & Noble when a man approached me by asking if I was looking for anything in particular. I said no and mentioning that I was just browsing, but the man continued to speak. He asked me if I was familiar with a particular author with whom a large number of people are knowledgeable. I said that I was. The man talked and talked about the same author. Now, that is all fine and well, but as I mentioned some related titles and similar authors, he hadn't a clue in the matter. This experience made me feel good that I knew as much, or more than a guy who was twice my age, because not only was I quoting text from *his* favorite author, but from a handful of the authors that were lining the shelves that day. It pays to diversify your reading and can also be a little fun.

Brownies and Kool-Aid: A Personal Story

I had the opportunity during my freshman year in college to attend a speech by Virginia Thomas, the wife of Supreme Court Justice Clarence Thomas, as she was a graduate of Creighton University School of Law. Afterward, I had the opportunity to get a brownie and some Kool-Aid and share a moment with Justice Thomas. I asked him what advice he had for college students, and he responded by saying, "You can either party and have fun for the next four years and pay for it the rest of your life, or you can pay for it now and party and have fun for the rest of your life; the choice is up to you." I prefer the latter.

A Philosophy or Two

Recent conversations about business and success with my friend Brandon Mason brought to my attention a very important philosophy that I now strive to live by. Brandon related an example of how people judge the success of others. People can look at someone and say, "Gee, that person must be a good student because he or she goes to a great school. Or, on the other hand, someone can say that that school is great because that person goes there." Much the same in one's professional career in that someone could say that Tom or Jane are successful because they work for Great Company XYZ. Or people could, and should, say that Great Company XYZ is great because Tom or Jane work there.

Mentors

This book has touched upon tapping into one's personal resources to learn and gain all there is out in the world relating to personal and professional success. However, I think that the word *mentor* should be used. Supplement it any way you like. I am unsure as to what Webster's terms a mentor, but call it what you will. Okay, I'll call it. A mentor is someone who has been there and done that. They want nothing but the best for you but realize the struggles ahead that you will have to face. This does not always mean the situation of the grandfather fishing with his grandson discussing the joys of life, but could simply apply to an older brother teaching his younger brother how to throw a baseball or an older sister giving advice to a younger sister on boys. Whatever the case may be, personally or professionally, mentors care for your future and are most often willing to do all in their power to ensure the success of that future. Find a mentor. Call him or her your mentor. Have more than one mentor. Most important, be a mentor to someone else.

Anticipation

This is kind of a crazy thing to think about, but I believe that it is quite beneficial in its actions. Anticipation means to simply be aware of what might become or what might take place. Most often I use the example of keeping a drink in your left hand when at a networking conference or a party because you will most likely have to shake someone's hand or give a high-five. That's anticipation. Surely this is not a deep definition by any means of the word, but provides a basis for thinking that can help achieve quite a bit when others fail to anticipate. Another example is just keeping track of your actions. Say that you are walking down the street and you have a cold. You might eventually have to "hawk one." Sure, it is understood that these things happen, but just anticipate who might be driving or walking by, or looking out the window at you. You would feel pretty lousy if you were to launch one when the girl you like is riding by or when a businessman you have been waiting to meet approaches you. These may seem small, but this is where it starts. Anticipation moves into all aspects of business. It could be anything from anticipating conversation topics during and after a meeting or anticipating the proper attire for an interview to anticipating how market trends will affect the industry you wish to someday enter. Anticipation. It is a good thing.

A Teacher Once Told Me . . .

When gathering feedback for this book, my former Spanish teacher, Kathy Scott, told me that I need to have a portion of this book that allows the readers to actually do something about what they have read. Teaching I suppose, in the simplest of efforts. It never hurts to apply the things you have read and heard about. Therefore, keeping in good standing with my former teacher and friend, I would like to suggest that you take a moment, upon finishing this book, or during your actual reading, to jot down things such as:

- My personal resources
- People I would like to contact
- CEOs I would like to take to lunch
- Organizations to get involved with
- Clothes I need
- Skills I have
- Skills I need to develop and improve upon
- Mentors I have
- Mentors I would like to have
- People I can be a mentor for
- Disciplines (remember the key to success)

Take Care of Yourself

Taking care of yourself is vitally important to attaining and maintaining professional and personal success. There is a saying that points out that if you want something done, give it to the busiest person, because busy people are excellent time managers and will find the time. Certainly one could say that it is wiser to give the task to the lazy person with all the time in the world, but think of the outcome. If the lazy person has been lazy, chances are they will remain lazy, both in the time it takes to complete the task and the overall result of the task itself.

Eating right and dressing well will improve your morale and increase your chances of staying healthy. This is important because the more and more involved someone gets, the more rundown their body becomes. Taking a run, going for a swim or row, or even doing some weight training are all great methods for keeping in shape and relieving stress, as well as improving personal appearance, mental toughness, and overall energy. It is important to have balance in your life.

Create Your Own Agenda

Creating your own agenda can certainly lead to career enjoyment and success. People are faced with three different agendas, the created-for-you-agenda, the half-agenda, and the create-your-own-agenda.

The created-for-you-agenda is what is most often found in the school system. Students have their work and plans laid out for them. Tasks and schedules are predetermined. Certainly this agenda can be fun and enjoyable at times, because there is no stress of figuring anything out for oneself. However, this agenda can become quite limiting and frustrating for those with bigger and brighter aspirations.

The half-agenda is most common, both in secondary education and the current business marketplace. Students in college have a wide range of classes they can choose from just the same as people largely have the freedom to pick and choose where they will work, dependent upon where they interview. However, once in a class or a job, there are certain rules, regulations, and procedures that need to be followed, as well as tasks and assignments to be completed. Once again, this can be a lot of fun, but can also be constraining at the same time.

Think of what it was like to be a kid. There were no timetables. You played in the dirt and rode around in puddles with no cares. The only thing you knew was to be home either by the noon whistle or when the sun was setting. When you were a kid, you created your own agenda. Think of how liberating that was at that time in your life. Think of how much fun you had and how much you could accomplish in a day. You could build a city in the sandbox, play football at the sandlot, go swimming all afternoon, and play kick the can or ditch in the evenings. The same philosophy applies to those enjoying career success today. Those persons, for the large part, create their own agendas. By doing so, they are able to accomplish a lot more in a day and are much happier doing so. It might take being in an executive position to achieve such an agenda-setting mentality, but it is certainly nothing to shy away from. Build a castle in the sand, begin a company, or become the chief executive by creating your own agenda. Just be home by sundown.

Last-Ditch Effort

- Look around at what you have. Learn to identify all the resources that you possess and begin to consult them. You will be amazed at how many you have and how willing they are to contribute to your pursuit of success, especially at a young age.
- Talk to people. Have a mentor or mentors. It never hurts to establish new relationships. Create your network of young and older people alike. Gather many perspectives from different viewpoints and you will surely be on the path to not only getting your foot in the door, but knocking it down altogether.
- Make appearances. See and be seen at the same time. Put your best foot forward. Go into every situation willing to make the effort toward your personal and professional success.
- Research companies. It pays to be in the know. Those who do are few and far between but are far more likely to capitalize on opportunities that come their way.
- Keep your head up. So maybe you do not have all the resources. Go make some. The thing to keep in mind is that by getting in early and achieving the know-how, you are already putting yourself ahead of so many others. That alone should make you smile and allow yourself to bounce back from any little hitches you may encounter.
- Get a business card, plain and simple. Be sure that you have them available for easy access. Carry some in your cardholder, your wallet, car, suit pocket, or anywhere else.

- There are a lot of successful people out there in the business world. My philosophy is that I can either say, "Wow, if that idiot can do it, so can I," *or I can* say, "Wow, if that really successful person, who is really admired and respected, can do it, then so can I." I prefer the latter, and that is how I wrote this book and try to live my life.
- As author and professional speaker John C. Maxwell says, "Those who are successful focus more on what they are doing right, rather on what they are doing wrong." Try it sometime.
- "Act as if." Yes, this is from the movie *Boiler Room*, but it is so true. You are who you want to be and you ought to want to be successful.

Embrace life, have confidence in yourself, take action.
— ANONYMOUS

You! Yes, You!

So, what makes me so special? What have I done that has made me successful? Well, I hope that through reading this you will have picked up on some of the things that I have done in terms of getting my foot in the door and networking. If that does not convince you, then why don't you give me a call sometime, or shoot me an e-mail, and we can chat. However, it is not the point of this book for me to rant and rave about this, that, and the other. The point is to tell you that *you* have what it takes to be successful. Yes, you. It is important that *you* note what *you* have done in *your* life. Don't just look at what you have done, however, but at what you *will* do. Think of all the pages of a book that you could fill with both past and future successes, or maybe even failures and how you grew from them.

Seek not outside yourself, success is within.
— MARY LOU COOK

Get off Your Butt

Get off your butt. Put down this book and go make it happen. You have the knowledge and the skills that put you above those who do not, but that is not good enough in this case. You must apply your knowledge to surpass those who are already in the know.

Joy is when anticipation meets action.
— ANONYMOUS

Dan Harbeke's Favorite Resources

Great Books

Beware the Naked Man Who Offers You His Shirt, Harvey Mackay

Dealing with an Angry Public, Patrick Field and Lawrence Susskind

Dig Your Well Before You're Thirsty, Harvey Mackay

Don't Send a Resume, Jeffrey J. Fox

Five Temptations of a CEO, Patrick Lencioni

How to Become a CEO, Jeffrey J. Fox

Iacocca, Lee Iacocca

Richest Man in Babylon, George S. Clason

The Secret Handshake, Kathleen Kelley Reardon

Selling the Invisible, Harry Beckwith

Straight to the Top, Paul G. Stern

Swim with the Sharks without Being Eaten Alive, Harvey Mackay

What They Don't Teach You at Harvard Business School,
Mark H. McCormick

Favorite Websites

www.sellingtobigcompanies.com

www.theacorngroup.com

www.bgiinc.com

www.unlockingthesecrets.com

www.strausclothing.com

www.mackay.com

www.mhproofreaders.com

www.bachrach.com

www.forbes.com

www.fortune.com

Best Networking Organizations

Chamber of Commerce

Jaycees

Knights of Columbus

Rotary International

Toastmasters

Afterword

Get In! itself came about in such a way that networking made it possible. I just happened to be in Sydney, Australia, the Christmas break of my freshman year in college. I was a junior counselor for the first ever International Student Representative Conference. I found out about the conference from having attended the National Association of Student Council's National Leadership Camp (NLC) at Outlaw Ranch, Custer, South Dakota, the summer before my senior year in high school. I later returned to counsel there for two summers, an opportunity which is still paying huge dividends. On the last day of the conference, I was walking and talking with Rocco Marano, the head of all student council's and National Honor Societies in the United States. We were talking about a book that I had made for my senior class during my last year in high school and how I had even given out nearly one hundred copies while counseling at NLC. I gave Rocco a copy and told him that one day I would like to write my own book. Rocco mentioned that he had a colleague named Dr. Tom Koerner, whom he used to work with and who is now at ScarecrowEducation. On what I was going to write about I did not yet know, but I knew I would want to put out a book in the near future.

So it was, the summer after my sophomore year in college that I called on Rocco for the name of his friend. Sure enough he came through and within a day I had made the contact and so began the process for putting the book together. A simple story on how this book came to be that no doubt displays the power of, and achievement possible through, networking and getting your foot in the door at a young age.

About the Author

Dan Harbeke is a young man from West Fargo, North Dakota, who is currently completing his studies in marketing and political science at Creighton University in Omaha, Nebraska. Dan plans on studying overseas, eventually obtaining an M.B.A and becoming a consultant, corporate executive, and politician.

Harbeke has worked in numerous facets of business, the most notable being the Chamber of Commerce of Fargo Moorhead, the Greater Omaha Chamber of Commerce, and New York Life Insurance Company. He has served as president of the Delta Pi chapter of the professional business fraternity Alpha Kappa Psi, a counselor at National Leadership Camps, and an International Guide to the first ever International Student Representative Conference in Sydney, Australia. Harbeke has also compiled works and produced a book earlier in his high school career. He has been the keynote speaker on numerous occasions for various Chamber and Youth Court functions and is active in Rotary International.